Contents

Audit Report

Appendices

Abbreviations

Fiscal Service	Bureau of the Fiscal Service
IP	Internet Protocol
IT	Information Technology
NIST SP	National Institute of Standards and Technology Special Publication
OCC	Office of the Comptroller of the Currency
OIG	Treasury Office of Inspector General
PII	Personally Identifiable Information
TNet	Treasury Network

OIG

The Department of the Treasury
Office of Inspector General

October 17, 2013

Thomas J. Curry
Comptroller of the Currency

This report represents the results of our audit of network and systems security at the Office of the Comptroller of the Currency (OCC). Our objective was to determine whether sufficient protections exist to prevent and detect unauthorized access into OCC's network and systems.

To accomplish our objective, we performed a series of internal and external vulnerability assessments and penetration tests on OCC's workstations, servers, network-attached peripherals (such as cameras and printers), infrastructure devices, and Internet websites. We also tested the physical security of OCC's headquarters and performed social engineering tests by e-mail and phone phishing.[1] Additionally, we followed up on the findings in our prior report from 2008.[2] Due to the time that has passed since our prior report, we did not determine if the findings that are repeated in this report were issues that had been resolved and then deteriorated back to the initial condition, or if they were long standing issues that had not been addressed. We performed our fieldwork in Washington, DC, in February and March 2013. Our objective, scope, and methodology are described in more detail in appendix 1.

Results in Brief

We determined that OCC's security measures were not sufficient to fully prevent and detect unauthorized access into

---

[1] Phishing is a fraud method where the perpetrator uses what appears to be official communication such as e-mail or phone calls in an attempt to gather information from recipients.
[2] OIG, *Information Technology: Network Security at the Office of the Comptroller of the Currency Needs Improvement*, OIG-08-035 (June 3, 2008)

its network and systems by internal threats,[3] or external threats[4] that gained an internal foothold. Also, OCC's security measures were not adequate to fully protect personally identifiable information (PII) from Internet-based threats. On a positive note, we found that physical security at OCC's new headquarters location was adequate.

Our test results revealed that not all required security controls were consistently applied over OCC's network and systems. To test for weaknesses in controls intended to thwart internal threats, we were given the typical access provided to any OCC employee — OCC access badges, an OCC-issued laptop computer, and a local network account, as well as network access for Treasury Office of Inspector General (OIG) test laptops. Using OIG test laptops, configured with network assessment and penetration tools, we discovered factory-preset default usernames and passwords were being used on several systems. With that knowledge, we exploited the systems with our penetration test tool and found clear text passwords that allowed us to log onto several systems using local and network administrative accounts. Once we had access to these administrative accounts, we created a domain administrator account for ourselves. With this account, we had full control of every OCC computer. We had permissions to do anything on any computer, from viewing what was running on users' desktops to saving and deleting files on file servers to adding and deleting accounts on the domain controller.

In performing another test on internal threats, we used employee information posted on OCC's intranet and available to all OCC employees. With that information, we were able to impersonate an OCC employee and convince OCC's Help Desk to reset that employee's password, thereby giving us full access to the user's account.

---

[3] An internal or insider threat is a current or former employee, contractor, or other business partner who has or had authorized access to a network, system, or data, and intentionally exceeds or misuses that access, resulting in a negative effect on the organization's information security.
[4] An external threat is a threat originating outside the organization.

To illustrate examples of weaknesses in controls intended to thwart external threats, we prepared and sent spoofed e-mails to OCC users using an e-mail client[5] on an OIG laptop computer to connect to OCC's e-mail server through the Internet. This server was operated by the Bureau of the Fiscal Service (Fiscal Service) on behalf of OCC. Also, we successfully downloaded through the Internet on an OIG laptop, PII from a public web server owned and managed by OCC. The outcomes of these tests are explained in our findings later in this report.

We consider the breadth, depth, and potential impact of the network security deficiencies as serious matters that require prompt corrective action by OCC management. In all, we are reporting seven findings:

1. Default usernames and passwords were present in OCC's systems
2. OCC did not fully implement least privilege controls
3. PII on OCC's public-facing web server was vulnerable to unauthorized access
4. OCC's e-mail servers were vulnerable to spoofed e-mail (Repeat Finding)
5. OCC's configuration management needs improvement (Repeat Finding)
6. OCC's Help Desk was susceptible to social engineering attacks
7. OCC's patch and version management needs improvement (Repeat Finding)

We are making 11 recommendations to address these findings.

In a written response to a draft copy of this report, OCC management concurred with our findings and recommendations, and provided its corrective actions taken and planned (see appendix 2). OCC's stated and planned corrective actions are responsive to the intent of our recommendations.

---

[5] An email client is a computer program used to access an email server.

Background

OCC was created by Congress to charter national banks, to oversee a nationwide system of banking institutions, and to assure that national banks are safe and sound, competitive and profitable, and capable of serving in the best possible manner the banking needs of their customers. OCC's network and systems are integral parts of its mission support structure. Several OCC systems contain PII collected during examinations and other oversight activities. As a federal agency, OCC is prohibited by law from releasing PII to the public.

Because OCC's computers are connected with each other, other bureaus' networks, and the Internet, it is important that proper configurations and controls be in place to ensure that only authorized users are granted access. Unauthorized access to OCC's network could provide an intruder with the opportunity to compromise the confidentiality, integrity, and availability of sensitive information. Once inside, unauthorized users could extract, delete, or modify sensitive data; discover user names and passwords; and launch denial-of-service attacks. If these unauthorized activities are not prevented or timely detected, such activities could result in compromises of information and systems, and thus hinder OCC's mission.

Findings and Recommendations

Finding 1   Default Usernames and Passwords Were Present in OCC's Systems

We found that default factory-preset administrative usernames and passwords were present in OCC's systems. In one test we conducted, we discovered a default username and password of an internal service account on an OCC server which had local administrator privileges. We used those privileges and deployed our penetration test tool's agents to the host server. That server contained password hashes[6] for local and domain administrator accounts. Using these hashes, we obtained a domain administrator's password, which we then used to log on to the network domain controller.[7] With full access given to a typical domain administrative account, we created a domain administrator account and thereby had full control of OCC's network.

During a different test, we were able to access a management console[8] on an OCC website by using a default factory-preset password. Using the information from the console, we gained access to PII. The details of PII access are described in Finding 3.

In another test, we discovered and used factory-preset usernames and passwords for local administrative accounts to access printers, Internet Protocol (IP) cameras, IP camera servers, network infrastructure devices, and voice-over-IP devices. Each account provided full control of the device, including the capability to change configuration, accounts, and data on the device.

National Institute of Standards and Technology Special Publication (NIST SP) 800-53, Revision 3, "Recommended Security Controls for Federal Information Systems," requires organizations to manage passwords for users and devices by changing the default password upon installation. Furthermore, OCC's Master Security Control Catalog, v2.0.1, dated December 2012, requires that all default account passwords be changed.

OCC staff stated that their "common practice" is to change default usernames and passwords. After being briefed on our

---

[6] A password hash is the result of a password that has been transformed into another string of alphanumeric characters by a one-way algorithm (i.e., you cannot recover the original password by simply using the hash).

[7] Domain controllers are computers that use one shared directory to store security and user-account information for an entire Windows domain.

[8] A management console is a tool that allows someone to modify information, passwords, and system settings.

findings, they informed us that they scanned a sample of network assets but were unable to find any system or machine configured with default passwords. They also said that the passwords on the IP cameras were not changed because the cameras were low-risk to OCC. We did not receive any documentation of this "common practice" that would make it a standard procedure, nor were we provided with the sample that OCC staff scanned.

By leaving default usernames and passwords unchanged, those who pose a threat to information technology (IT) security could easily access OCC's network and systems. The aggregate effect of the presence of these default usernames and passwords is that attackers could have unrestricted access to these devices and the data stored on them, especially the password hash for local and domain administrative accounts.

In accordance with our Rules of Engagement, we did not attempt to perform actions that would disrupt OCC's operations, such as deleting data, powering off servers or other resources, locking out accounts, and similar activities, any of which could have resulted in interruption or shutdown of devices or services. However, malicious attackers would have no such restrictions against performing these actions.

Recommendations

We recommend that the Comptroller of the Currency:

1. Develop and implement a standard procedure requiring default usernames and passwords be changed on all systems and devices.

Management Response

OCC updated its standard operating procedures in June 2013 to provide guidance that will ensure that all default user names and passwords are changed on all systems and devices. The updated standard operating procedures require all devices to be subject to management controls, which include specific checks in the review and approval process to ensure that usernames and passwords are changed prior to introducing new or modified software and/or devices to the network.

<u>OIG Comment</u>

Management's stated corrective action is responsive to our recommendation.

2. Change all default usernames and passwords on all systems and devices in an expeditious manner.

<u>Management Response</u>

All default usernames and passwords were changed or updated effective September 2, 2013.

<u>OIG Comment</u>

Management's stated corrective action is responsive to our recommendation.

3. Periodically review accounts to detect default usernames and passwords on all systems and devices, and, when detected, change them.

<u>Management Response</u>

Effective August 16, 2013, OCC began monthly scans to identify default user names and passwords on software and network devices which results in a Default Credentials report. In addition, OCC also conducts a Network Penetration Test every other month producing the Network Penetration Test report. These reports identify default usernames and passwords across network devices. OCC immediately remediates any findings. Results are periodically reported to the OCC Chief Information Officer and other OCC IT officials.

OIG Comment

Management's stated corrective action is responsive to our recommendation.

Finding 2   OCC Did Not Fully Implement Least Privilege Controls

We observed that OCC had not implemented least privilege controls[9] in a way that effectively restricted our ability, or an attacker's ability, to launch attacks within OCC's network. We noted that OCC's network is "flat," meaning that it lacks subnets and partitions that restrict access. Consequently, there is an increased risk that attacks could spread easily and rapidly throughout a "flat network." Over the course of our audit, we successfully compromised OCC workstations, servers, and other network-attached devices. From our workstations, we were able to compromise OCC systems in Tulsa, Wichita, New York, and Washington, D.C.; OCC systems used by business units, including the Office of the Ombudsman; and OCC systems used by its examiners in a number of locations. We also discovered that many systems were configured with the same local administrative password. The situation was compounded because of an extraordinarily high number of domain administrator accounts on the network's domain controller. In addition to a higher than expected number of domain administrators, we found that a number of service accounts had far greater administrative privileges than should have been necessary for such accounts.[10]

NIST SP 800-53, Revision 3, "Recommended Security Controls for Federal Information Systems," requires organizations employ the concept of least privilege and only allow access necessary to accomplish assigned tasks in accordance with organizational missions and business functions.

---

[9] The principle of least privilege is the practice of allowing only access at the minimal level that will allow normal business functions to take place. This translates to giving people and processes the lowest level of rights available that allow them to still do their jobs.

[10] A service account is a user account that is created explicitly to provide a security context (i.e., privileges and restrictions) for services running on a server, as opposed to a human user.

An OCC official stated that the network functions met the needs of the organization and access to network assets was appropriately restricted. The official also noted that OCC's network did not restrict traffic between physical locations or business units. That said, we were also informed that OCC personnel have not performed a risk analysis of a "flat network" as compared to a more internally segmented one.

Because systems and devices connected to OCC's internal network could freely communicate between one another, with very little internal partitioning, we successfully attacked multiple OCC systems in a very short amount of time from a single workstation. OCC's "flat network" configuration allowed us to reuse password hashes we found on previously compromised machines and to gather more information using compromised devices. Moreover, the "flat network" increased the attack surface by giving us easy access to the entire network once a foothold on any system was established. As a result, OCC's failure to segment the network and implement least privilege enabled us to move through the network unimpeded. Furthermore, OCC's practice of using the same local administrator passwords contributed to the speed and ease with which we compromised systems on the network. The use of factory default passwords allowed for much of the same. Finally, having a large number of unnecessary domain administrator accounts increased risks of attackers targeting and exploiting powerful accounts and account holders.

Recommendations

We recommend that the Comptroller of the Currency:

1. Conduct a risk assessment of OCC's network topology and implement appropriate least privilege controls.

    Management Response

    OCC will complete a comprehensive assessment to quantify the risks and gaps associated with the legacy "flat" network topology, and will develop a network topology architecture and roadmap for enabling appropriate least privilege controls by December 31, 2013.

Management's planned corrective actions are responsive to our recommendation.

2. Restrict network access as required by business needs and in accordance with risk assessment results and least privilege principles.

Management Response

OCC strengthened its policies, procedures, and network scanning for managing accounts with elevated privileges. These changes mandate that elevated privileges are granted based on specific roles and subjected to a multi-tiered review and approval adjudication process. The domain administrator accounts have been adjudicated and rationalized. Other relevant accounts will be rationalized by December 15, 2013, and service accounts will be rationalized by March 31, 2014. OCC will execute an approved network topology architecture and roadmap to restrict network access in accordance with business needs and least privilege principles by March 17, 2014.

OIG Comment

Management's stated and planned corrective actions are responsive to our recommendation.

Finding 3

PII on OCC's Public-Facing Web Server Was Vulnerable to Unauthorized Access

We found that PII was vulnerable to unauthorized access on OCC's Internet website, ComplaintReferralExpress.gov. This is a web-based system that allows OCC and other state and federal regulators and offices to exchange consumer complaints about institutions they do not supervise. We were able to use a factory-preset username and password for the website's management console to modify system settings and gather sensitive information. Among the information found on this server, we were able to gather names of bank customers who had filed complaints and their associated phone numbers, street addresses, and e-mail addresses.

The Privacy Act requires federal agencies to establish appropriate administrative, technical, and physical safeguards to protect the security and confidentiality of records about individuals. Additionally, OCC entered into Memoranda of Understanding with state and federal agencies that require OCC maintain appropriate safeguards to protect non-public and confidential information.

OCC officials stated that they were not aware that the website's management console was available to the Internet.

Failure to provide adequate protections for PII on the ComplaintReferralExpress.gov website could allow attackers to obtain bank customers' personal information for malicious intent.

Recommendation

We recommend that the Comptroller of the Currency implement safeguards to protect PII on OCC's Internet website.

Management Response

OCC changed the default password on the website on April 24, 2013 and decoupled the management console from the publicly facing website on May 28, 2013. To ensure these websites remain secure, OCC runs monthly vulnerability scans that detect weaknesses. In summary, OCC (1) updated its policy and procedures for securing websites with PII; (2) implemented tools and manual testing to conduct monthly security testing of all of its external websites; and (3) tested the specific method the auditors used to exploit the website to ensure it could not be reproduced on any other OCC websites.

OIG Comment

Management's stated corrective actions are responsive to our recommendation.

| Finding 4 | **OCC's E-mail Servers Were Vulnerable to Spoofed E-mail (Repeat Finding)** |

We found that OCC's e-mail servers allowed unauthenticated e-mails to be sent to any of OCC's e-mail users from outside of Treasury with a spoofed occ.treas.gov source address. As a result, we successfully sent from an OIG laptop, spoofed e-mails to OCC e-mail users with forged OCC e-mail headers so that the message appeared to have been originated from within OCC. This vulnerability was previously identified in our 2008 report.

Treasury Directive Publication 85-01, "Treasury Information Technology Security Program," requires all inbound e-mail with a sender address claiming to be from a Treasury entity to be verified as having originated from a trusted Treasury e-mail system.

An OCC official provided us with the Interconnection Security Agreement where OCC agreed to have Fiscal Service manage its inbound e-mail traffic from the Internet to its servers. We discussed the vulnerability in the e-mail servers with OCC and Fiscal Service personnel, and OCC officials stated they would work with Fiscal Service to resolve the issue.

If mail servers allow e-mails to be sent without authentication, there is an increased risk of servers being exploited by attackers by sending malicious e-mails or spam. Spoofed e-mails, as described above, appear legitimate and lend credibility to phishing attacks.

Recommendation

We recommend that the Comptroller of the Currency work with Fiscal Service to ensure controls are put in place to prevent spoofed e-mails from being sent to or through OCC servers.

Management Response

In consultation with Fiscal Service and OIG, OCC implemented an alternate strategy to address the identified vulnerability, and

OCC began blocking unauthorized source spoofing of the occ.treas.gov domain effective August 31, 2013.

OIG Comment

Management's stated corrective action is responsive to our recommendation.

Finding 5   **OCC's Configuration Management Needs Improvement (Repeat Finding)**

As part of our network and system security assessment, we performed network scans to detect systems, devices, and network services running on the OCC domain. We discovered 222 unique open ports[11] running network services on systems and devices throughout the network. This vulnerability was previously identified in our 2008 report.[12]

NIST SP 800-53, Revision 3, "Recommended Security Controls for Federal Information Systems," requires organizations restrict the use of ports, protocols, and services not required for business purposes. Additionally, it requires organizations to identify, document, and approve exceptions to the mandatory configuration settings. Organizations are required to monitor their systems and applications for changes to these configuration settings.

According to an OCC official, unauthorized software, ports and services discovered on workstations were likely installed or configured when OCC general users had administrative privileges on their workstations. The official stated that these privileges were removed in 2012 and OCC scanned for unnecessary ports and services at least annually. However, when we provided a sample of open ports and asked why they were open on servers, OCC officials could only provide us with the causes for some of these open ports. Furthermore, OCC

---

[11] A port is a means by which a program or service on one system can communicate with a program or service located on another system.
[12] OIG, *Information Technology: Network Security at the Office of the Comptroller of the Currency Needs Improvement*, OIG-08-035 (June 3, 2008)

officials could not provide us with approved business justifications for any of the open ports in our sample.

Allowing unnecessary open ports and services increases the attack surface available to attackers by permitting unmonitored and potentially vulnerable services to run on the network. These services provide an attacker with a wider array of potential vulnerabilities to exploit. Failure to monitor and document open ports and services makes it difficult for an organization to control and track changes to its environment, and provides a means by which an attacker could run malicious services undetected.

Recommendations

We recommend that the Comptroller of the Currency:

1. Develop and implement procedures to identify, document, and approve base configuration settings for ports and services.

   #### Management Response

   OCC's policy requires that mandatory configuration settings be established for information technology devices. To ensure consistent implementation of this policy, OCC will (1) complete a baseline comprehensive configuration document reflecting the OCC's business needs for using ports and services by September 30, 2013; (2) update the existing configuration management process to include the identification and documentation of essential ports and services for application and hardware changes effective October 31, 2013; and (3) continue its existing monitoring and assessment processes to verify compliance with the baseline configurations.

   #### OIG Comment

   Management's planned corrective actions are responsive to our recommendation.

2. Disable or remove unnecessary or unused services or open ports.

Management Response

New personal computers deployed OCC-wide in fiscal year 2013 restrict configuration changes and ability to install software, thereby limiting the desktop to approved-only open ports and services. By October 1, 2013, OCC will implement procedures to incorporate monthly monitoring and immediate disabling or removal of unauthorized ports and services for all network devices and applications; and by March 31, 2014, OCC will disable or remove all unnecessary or unused services or open ports identified by this audit.

OIG Comment

Management's planned corrective actions are responsive to our recommendation.

Finding 6

OCC's Help Desk Was Susceptible to Social Engineering Attacks

We found that OCC's Help Desk was susceptible to social engineering attacks. The standard procedure used by the Help Desk to verify a user's identity only required information that was available to all OCC users via OCC's internal network. Using available employee information, we impersonated an OCC employee and were able to convince Help Desk to reset the employee's password whom we impersonated. Once changed, we could have used that password to compromise the employee's account. Based on the success of our attempt combined with the Help Desk's use of a standard procedure to verify user identity, we decided to forgo further testing to minimize disruption to OCC users.

NIST SP 800-53, Revision 3, "Recommended Security Controls for Federal Information Systems," requires organizations to verify the identity of the individual receiving a new password.

OCC officials told us that they were unaware that the information used by the Help Desk to validate user identities was available to all OCC employees until we brought this issue to their attention.

Depending on whose account was targeted, an attacker could obtain a new password for a user account with access to administrative privileges or access to sensitive and privileged information. An attacker could also perform overt malicious activities while logged onto a legitimate user account with a fraudulently reset password. Once an attacker resets an account's password, the legitimate user of the account would not be able to log on to the account, until they requested a password reset.

Recommendation

We recommend that the Comptroller of the Currency improve the Help Desk's procedures for verification of user identities to prevent impersonation. The procedures should provide for verification of user identity information that is not available to others.

Management Response

On July 22, 2013, OCC implemented a new method for password reset which does not use information available to others. All users and OCC IT staff were informed of the changes, and internal controls within IT Customer Support were implemented to ensure compliance with the new policy.

OIG Comment

Management's stated corrective actions are responsive to our recommendation.

Finding 7   **OCC's Patch and Version Management Needs Improvement (Repeat Finding)**

We found 19 instances of unsupported or outdated versions of software (operating systems, database management systems, and web application servers) in use on OCC's network. Specifically, we found the following:

Operating Systems (13 instances found):

- 4 servers running Windows Server 2003 Service Pack 1, unsupported after April 2009.
- 4 workstations running Windows XP Service Pack 2, unsupported after July 2010.
- 5 servers running Debian Linux 4.0, unsupported after February 2012.

Database Management Systems (2 instances found):

- 1 server running Oracle MySQL 5.0.18. Oracle has announced that no new Maintenance Releases, Bug Fixes, Patches, and updates would be released as of January 2012.
- 1 server running Oracle MySQL 5.0.95. Oracle has announced that no new Maintenance Releases, Bug Fixes, Patches, and updates would be released as of January 2012.

Web Application Servers (4 instances found):

- 4 instances of a vulnerable web service (Apache Tomcat[13] 4.1.18-4.1.29). Tomcat 4.1.x was last updated June 2009 and it is no longer being updated by its developers. The current versions are 6.0.x, released in December 2006, and 7.0.x, released in January 2011.

With respect to the Operating Systems, OCC staff told us that their workstations were running fully supported Microsoft operating systems. However, when OCC staff conducted their own scan, it also identified four instances of Microsoft Windows XP Service Pack 2. They did not explain the presence of those instances in their scan. With respect to the other

---

[13] Apache Tomcat is a web server that is an open source software implementation of the Java Servlet and JavaServer Pages technologies.

operating systems, the Database Management Systems, and the Web Application Servers, OCC staff initially disagreed with the instances of outdated software identified by our scan, but later told us that the instances had been addressed through upgrades, decommissioning of the software, or determined they are not a security risk. We did not, as part of our audit, verify that these actions had been taken.

NIST SP 800-53, Revision 3, "Recommended Security Controls for Federal Information Systems and Organizations," states that organizations must promptly install security-relevant software updates (e.g., patches, service packs, and hot fixes).

This finding was previously identified in our 2008 report, and is a matter that requires continuous management attention. Systems running unsupported operating systems, database management systems, or web services do not and cannot receive patches or updates from the software providers in response to security threats from newly discovered vulnerabilities.

Recommendation

We recommend that the Comptroller of the Currency ensure that systems and applications are running supported and up-to-date operating systems.

Management Response

On June 6, 2013, OCC implemented a bi-weekly network scanning procedure for detecting instances of end-of-life software. By September 30, 2013, OCC will implement an end-of-life and unsupported software policy, and will implement procedures for upgrading software on workstations, servers, and network devices. By November 30, 2013, all instances of end-of-life software identified by this audit will be resolved.

OIG Comment

Management's stated and planned corrective actions are responsive to our recommendation.

* * * * * *

I would like to extend my appreciation to Edward Dorris, Chief Information Officer, and OCC staff for the cooperation and courtesies extended to my staff during the audit. If you have any questions, please contact me at 202-927-5171 or Larissa Klimpel, Information Technology Audit Manager, at 202-927-0361. Major contributors to this report are listed in appendix 3.

/s/

Tram Jacquelyn Dang
Audit Director

Our objective for this audit was to determine whether sufficient protections exist to prevent and detect unauthorized access into the Department of the Treasury Office of the Comptroller of the Currency's (OCC) network and systems.

To accomplish our objective, we performed a series of internal and external vulnerability assessments and penetration tests on OCC's workstations, servers, network-attached peripherals (such as cameras and printers), infrastructure devices, and Internet websites.

Internal assessments were performed on-site at OCC's new headquarters facility in Washington, DC, in February and March of 2013. The internal assessment was conducted inside OCC's network, behind Treasury Network (TNet[14]) firewalls, with full knowledge of OCC, and we were provided the same system access, physical assets, information, and other resources available to OCC employees stationed at headquarters. We also used Office of Inspector General (OIG) owned and licensed hardware and software, including Core Impact and Nexpose. During our tests, we notified OCC information security staff of issues we discovered that we believed may have been indicative of serious problems that would require their immediate attention. While at OCC headquarters, we performed social engineering tests by e-mail and phone phishing[15] to determine whether OCC's Help Desk was able to prevent and detect attempts at impersonating OCC employees. We also conducted limited tests of the physical security by attempting to enter the building from the outside without using OCC-issued badges. Lastly, we followed up on the status of the findings in our prior report from 2008.[16]

External assessments were performed from OIG headquarters via non-TNet connections and using only OIG hardware and software, and information available to the general public.

---

[14] TNet is a wide area network that provides Treasury with e-mail, Internet, and voice traffic applications.

[15] Phishing is a fraud method where the perpetrator uses what appears to be official communication such as e-mail or phone calls in an attempt to gather information from recipients.

[16] OIG, *Information Technology: Network Security at the Office of the Comptroller of the Currency Needs Improvement*, OIG-08-035 (June 3, 2008)

In accordance with the agreed-upon Rules of Engagement, we excluded TNet, as well as tests that could have adversely affected operations and may have resulted in denial of service to OCC employees or customers.

Upon completion of our tests, we provided OCC's Information Technology audit liaison with the reports generated by our automated assessment tools so that timely corrective actions could be taken. The reports provided details on specific vulnerabilities detected and exploited, and the tools' suggested actions necessary to address them. We also briefed OCC Information Technology management at the end of our on-site evaluation on our activities and access we gained over the course of our audit, including our analysis of the issues reported by the tools we used.

We conducted this performance audit in accordance with generally accepted government auditing standards. Those standards require that we plan and perform the audit to obtain sufficient, appropriate evidence to provide a reasonable basis for our finding and conclusions based on our audit objective. We believe that the evidence obtained provides a reasonable basis for our findings and conclusions based on our audit objective.

September 23, 2013

Ms. Tram Jacquelyn Dang
Audit Director
Office of Inspector General
Department of the Treasury
Washington, DC 20220

Subject: Response to Draft Report

Dear Ms. Dang:

We have reviewed your draft report titled "Information Technology: OCC's Network and Systems Security Controls Were Deficient." The report presents the results of the Office of Inspector General's (OIG) internal and external vulnerability assessments and penetration tests on OCC's network, systems and physical security.

You found that OCC's security measures were not sufficient to fully prevent and detect unauthorized access into its network and systems by internal threats or external threats that gained an internal foothold; security measures were not adequate to fully protect personally identifiable information (PII) from Internet-based threats. You did, however, find that physical security at the OCC's new headquarters is adequate. You make 11 recommendations to address the following deficiencies: use of default usernames and passwords; failure to fully implement least privilege controls; vulnerability of PII to unauthorized access; vulnerability of e-mail to spoofing; configuration management; vulnerability of Help Desk to social engineering; and patch and version management.

We concur with your findings and recommendations. The enclosed table outlines our actions to address them.

If you need additional information, please contact me or Ed Dorris, Chief Information Officer, at 202-649-6001.

Sincerely,

Thomas J. Curry
Comptroller of the Currency

Enclosure

OCC's Network and Systems Security Controls Were Deficient	
OIG Recommendation	**OCC Management Response**
#1 Develop and implement a standard procedure requiring default usernames and passwords be changed on all systems and devices.	Standard operating procedures (SOPs) were updated on June 6, 2013 to provide guidance that will ensure that all default user names and passwords are changed on all systems and devices. The updated SOPs require all devices to be subject to management controls, which include specific checks in the review and approval process to ensure that usernames and passwords are changed prior to introducing new or modified software and/or devices to the network.
#2 Change all default usernames and passwords on all systems and devices in an expeditious manner.	All default usernames and passwords were changed or updated effective September 2, 2013.
#3 Periodically review accounts to detect default usernames and passwords on all systems and devices, and when detected, change them.	Effective August 16, 2013, the OCC began monthly scans to identify default user names and passwords on software and network devices which results in a Default Credentials report. In addition, OCC also conducts a Network Penetration Test every other month producing the Network Penetration Test report. These reports identify default usernames and passwords across network devices. OCC immediately remediates any findings. Results are periodically reported to the CIO, Deputy CIOs, and IT director-level leadership.
#4 Conduct a risk assessment of OCC's network topology and implement appropriate least privilege controls.	The OCC will complete a comprehensive assessment to quantify the risks and gaps associated with the legacy "flat" network topology, and will develop a Target Network Topology Architecture and Roadmap for enabling appropriate least privilege controls by December 31, 2013.
#5 Restrict network access as required by business needs and in accordance with risk assessment results and least privilege principles.	OCC has strengthened its policies, procedures, and network scanning for managing accounts with elevated privileges (i.e., domain administrators, X-accounts, and service accounts). These changes mandate that elevated privileges are granted based on specific roles and subjected to a multi-tiered review and approval adjudication process. The domain administrator accounts have been adjudicated and rationalized. The X-accounts will be rationalized by December 15, 2013, and service accounts will be rationalized by March 31, 2014. OCC will execute the approved Target Network Topology Architecture and Roadmap to restrict network access in accordance with business needs and least privilege principles by March 17, 2014.

1

#6 Implement safeguards to protect PII on OCC's Internet website.	The default password for the Complaint Referral Express website was changed on April 24, 2013, and the management console for the Complaint Referral Express website was decoupled from the publicly facing link on May 28, 2013. All external OCC websites that contain Personally Identifiable Information (PII) are secured and are not at risk for data leakage. To ensure these sites remain secure, OCC runs monthly vulnerability scans that detect weaknesses. In summary, the OCC: 1) has updated its policy and procedures for securing sites with PII; 2) is using tools and manual testing to conduct monthly security testing of all of its external websites; and 3) has tested the specific method the auditors used to exploit the website to ensure it could not be reproduced on any other OCC websites.
#7 Work with Fiscal Service to ensure controls are put in place to prevent spoofed e-mails from being sent to or through OCC servers.	In consultation with the Treasury Bureau of Fiscal Service (BFS) and the OIG, the OCC implemented an alternate strategy to address the identified vulnerability, and the OCC began blocking unauthorized source spoofing of the occ.treas.gov domain effective August 31, 2013.
#8 Develop and implement procedures to identify, document, and approve base configuration settings for ports and services.	OCC has a specific policy that requires that mandatory configuration settings be established for information technology devices. To ensure consistent implementation of this policy, OCC will: 1) complete a baseline comprehensive configuration document reflecting the OCC's business needs for using ports and services by September 30, 2013; 2) update the existing configuration management process to include the identification and documentation of essential ports and services for application and hardware changes effective October 31, 2013; and 3) continue its existing monitoring and assessment processes to verify compliance with the baseline configurations.
#9 Disable or remove unnecessary or unused services or open ports.	New PCs deployed OCC-wide in FY13 restrict configuration changes and ability to install software, thereby limiting the desktop to approved-only open ports and services. By October 1, 2013, OCC will implement procedures to incorporate monthly monitoring and immediate disabling or removal of unauthorized ports and services for all network devices and applications; and by March 31, 2014, OCC will disable or remove all unnecessary or unused services or open ports identified in this audit. OCC is taking a methodical approach (based on rigorous testing) in order to mitigate disruption to business systems while disabling or removing unused services and ports across network devices and application portfolio.

2

#10 Improve the Help Desk's procedures for verification of user identities to prevent impersonation. The procedures should provide for verification of user identity information that is not available to others.	A new password authentication method for password reset, which does not use information available to others, was implemented on July 22, 2013. All users and OCC IT staff were informed of the changes, and internal controls within IT Customer Support were implemented to ensure compliance to the new policy.
#11 Ensure that systems and applications are running supported and up-to-date operating systems.	Effective June 6, 2013, OCC implemented a bi-weekly network scanning procedure for detecting and forecasting instances of end-of-life software; by September 30, 2013, OCC will implement the End-of-Life and Unsupported Software policy to manage end-of-life software within specified timeframes and will implement procedures for upgrading software on workstations, servers, and network devices; and all instances of end-of-life software identified in this audit will be resolved by no later than November 30, 2013.

3

Office of Information Technology (IT) Audits

Tram J. Dang, Audit Director
Larissa Klimpel, IT Audit Manager
Dan Jensen, Auditor-in-Charge
Jason Beckwith, IT Specialist
Mitul "Mike" Patel, IT Specialist
Don'te Kelley, IT Specialist
Jeanne DeGagne, Referencer

Office of the Comptroller of the Currency

Chief Information Officer

Department of the Treasury

Office of Chief Information Officer
Associate Chief Information Officer for Cyber Security
Office of Strategic Planning and Performance Management
Office of the Deputy Chief Financial Officer, Risk and Control
Group

Office of Management and Budget

Office of Inspector General Budget Examiner